Prayer in
Poetry
for the
Christian
Child

Bible Stories Told in Rhymes

Prayer in Poetry for the Christian Child

Bible Stories Told in Rhymes

by Vicky Andriotis

PUBLISHED BY
VICKY SPYROU-ANDRIOTIS
CONNECTICUT, USA

Published 2010 by
Vicky Spyrou-Andriotis

Printed and bound in the
United States of America
ISBN-10: 0-9821808-4-5
ISBN-13: 978-0-9821808-4-6

Prayer In Poetry For
The Christian Child
www.vickyandriotis.com

Cover and Book Design –
Vicky Spyrou-Andriotis

Written for our children, so that they might learn what is right and what is true, and grow to follow the teachings of our Lord.

Contents

"Let the little children come to Me, and do not forbid them; for of such is the kingdom of God."
Mark 10:14 NKJV™

Adam and Eve

Adam and Eve

Were the first of all
people
And they lived in the
Garden of Eden

The tree in the center

Made beautiful fruit
But God's rule was that
They could not eat them

A snake came along

Who was wicked and
wrong
And convinced them to
just have a bite

Eve picked from the tree

The apple looked sweet
And she thought
It would all be alright

Adam took a bite too

And right away knew
What they'd done
Must have been wrong

So God sent them away
Told them they couldn't
stay
For in Eden they did not
belong

–Genesis 3

Noah's Ark

A world without

kindness
A world without love
A world full of sin
Saddened God above

Only one man was

worthy
Only one to be saved
Only one whom God
trusted
So He called out his name

"Noah, make thee an

Ark
for the world will soon
end.
All the bad in it will vanish
So that you may begin
again."

Gather two of each

creature,
and your family too,
safely into your Ark
for the flood will come
soon."

And the earth was soon

covered
Forty days and forty
nights

On the Ark they would
drift
Knowing they'd be alright

When their journey was
done
A dove flew overhead
With a branch in his
mouth
"Must be land up ahead!"

God then made a
rainbow
As a promise to His friend
That He would never
destroy
The Earth that way again
—Genesis 6:9

Moses and the Ten Commandments

There once was a man

named Moses
Who led his people from
Egypt
For there they were only
slaves
And Moses wanted to
free them

So he led them far away

'til they came to the
Desert of Sanai
Where they camped
beneath a mountain
That God then told Moses
to climb

At the top God made

commandments
Rules, carved into a stone
And these tablets Moses
carried
Down the mountain all
alone

God had said

"I am your God,
the one and only
I am He.
Don't make statues
thinking they are gods.
That would truly bother
Me."

66"**W**hen you need to use
My name,
Do it only with respect.
And one day you will
keep holy.
That day, you will call the
Sabbath."

66"**B**e good always to

your parents.
Never kill a human being.
Be faithful to each other.
And don't ever steal a
thing."

You should never, ever

lie, or be jealous of your
friend's things."
And these rules Moses
explained
And he prayed for all their
sins

—*Exodus 19 & 20*

21

The Christmas Story

In Bethlehem

A child was born
To His mother, Mary
And God's only Son

King of Kings

And the light of the world
There was a great joy
When the news was
heard

Three kings who knew
And searched from afar
Found baby Jesus
When they followed a star

He lay in a manger
For there was no room at
the inn
He was sent by God, the
Father
To save us from sin

The kings brought Him
gifts
Gold, Frankincense, and
Myrrh
For He was our Savior
Of this they were sure

So they worshipped and
rejoiced
Then went on their way
And that is the story
Of the First Christmas Day
– *Luke 2*

When Jesus Was Baptized

On the Jordan River

Was a man named John
The son of Mother Mary's
cousin

He was sent by God

To prepare the way
And tell how God will
forgive all sins

"Be baptized," he said

"Be sorry. Be true.
Change, while there is still
time."

And so people came
From near and far
To confess their sins and
lies

One day Jesus came
To be baptized too
Just to show the will of
God

And though John was
confused
He was told what to do
And so Jesus was
baptized by John

Then the sky opened
wide
With the Spirit of God
inside
Which came down in the
shape of a dove

"This is My son

with whom I Am
pleased." Said God,
Whose voice came from
above. *Matthew 3*

The Disciples

As He walked by the Sea
of Galilee
Jesus came upon two
fishermen
"Simon Peter, Andrew,
leave your nets and
come."
So they went on to follow
Him

James and John- two
brothers in a boat
While preparing their
fishing nets
Heard Jesus calling out to
them both
So they left their things
and went

Levi, also known as

Matthew, was a tax
collector when
Jesus saw him and said,
"Follow Me."
Matthew did just that right
then

Later on when he found

Philip
Bartholomew, Thomas,
and James
Thaddeus, Simon, and
Judas
All followed Him just the
same

Together they preached

and healed
Together they followed
and believed
Together they witnessed
and taught
About everything they
had seen —*John 1*

The Man Who Couldn't Walk

The Paralytic Healed

There was a man
Who had been sick
For many, many years

And near this man
Were many more
Just waiting to be healed

For an angel came
At certain times
To a pool inside their
town

30

And he stirred the water
in such a way
That it cured the first to
step down

Now, that man who'd
been sick so many years
Had no one to carry him
in

When Jesus asked,
"Do you want to be
healed?"
That man said to Him

"I do, but have no one
who will help me to the
pool."

So Jesus said "Rise up
and walk."
And as if his legs were
new

He picked up the pallet
he'd been lying on
And went on to spread
the Good News
　　　　　—John 5

Sermon on the Mount & The Lord's Prayer

Upon the mountain

Where Jesus stood
People gathered near

Because the Lord

Had much to say
And they all wanted to
hear

First He said

"Love everyone,
Friends and enemies
alike.
Pray for them,
One and all.
It's easy if you try."

He told them not to

worry
What to eat, what to
drink,
What to wear
For God the Father knows
our needs,
And for us He will care

And then some people

asked him,
"Jesus, how do we pray?"
He replied, "There's no
need to babble. You
should always pray this
way:

Our Father Who art in

Heaven
Hallowed be Thy name
Thy Kingdom come
Thy Will be done
On Earth as it is in Heaven
Give us this day our daily
bread
And forgive us our
trespasses
As we forgive those who
trespass against us
And lead us not into
temptation
But deliver us from evil."

—Matthew

Even Storms
Obey

While on a boat
With His Disciples
Jesus fell asleep

But as He slept
The wind stirred up
And waves began to leap

Inside the boat
The water filled
As the waves crashed up
and down

The Disciples feared

With such a storm
That they were sure to
drown

"Wake up!"

They said to Jesus
"Can't you see that we're
afraid?"

And as Jesus calmed

the storm
He said, "Where is your
faith?"

—Luke 8

Five Loaves of Bread

Feeding the 5,000

Many people followed
Jesus
To hear what he had to
say
And one day they
followed him
To a place far, far away

As the day turned into
night
And the time had come to
eat
They would send them
back to town
To find the food they'd
need

But Jesus said, "Don't
go.
Don't we have something
for them?"
The Disciples told Him,
"No. Just two fish and
five loaves of bread.

It's not enough for all five
thousand.
It's not enough for even
ten."
But He made them all sit
down
While He blessed and
broke the bread

And the fish He broke in

pieces
And along with all the
bread
He placed it in the baskets
And gave it all to them

And they had so much

to eat
That they gathered up
again
Twelve baskets of
leftovers
From what Jesus gave to
them

—*Matthew 14*

Jesus Heals the Blind Man

There was a man
Who was born blind
Whom Jesus met one day

Jesus put spit
And dirt on his eyes
And told him to wash it
away

The man then arrived
At the pool of Siloam
And did as he was told

His eyes opened wide
He was no longer blind
What a miracle to behold!

Now the Pharisees
Who were strict with the
law
Were angry, and had
much to say

Because they believed
Only sinners could do
Miracles on the Sabbath
day

But the blind man said
"I was blind, but now see.
How can this be a sin?"

With a scream and a
shout
They threw him out
And he went on to
worship Him

—John 9

Lazarus

In a place called
Bethany
Outside of
Jerusalem
Lived
Martha,
Mary,
and
Lazarus
Whom
Jesus
called His
friends

One day
Lazarus
fell ill
And to
Jesus
a message
was
sent

That He should come
quickly, For his death He
could prevent

Jesus knew God had a
plan
So He didn't go that day
And by the time He had
arrived
Lazarus had passed away

Jesus told the sister,
Martha
That Lazarus would rise
again
And she went and called
Mary
Who cried when she saw
their friend

They led Jesus to the
tomb
Where Lazarus was
placed
And they rolled away the
stone
That was in the doorway

And he called,
"Lazarus, come out!"
And rising from his death
Lazarus walked out of his
tomb
Alive, once again

Jesus then thanked God
above
For God's Power
was proved that day
Even over death
For Lazarus rose
And lived again

—John 11

Jesus Saves Us

Jesus was sent
By God above
To save us with
His words and love

He came to wash us
Of our sins
By taking the punishment
For all of them

When the time came

For Him to go
The Disciple, called Judas
Was the one who told

And the soldiers came

And arrested Him
And placed Him on a
cross
Where He died for our
sins

But three days went by

And his friends went to
the tomb
Where they thought
Jesus lay
But they'd find out soon

That the tomb was

empty
For Jesus rose from the
dead
And later ascended to
Heaven
Just as He had said

Thankful

A prayer

O Lord, Jesus Christ

In Heaven above
How thankful I am
To know Your love

It's in the stars

And the grass at my feet
In the arms of my family
And those who care for
me

It's in those who are kind

And the friends that I love
And I'm thankful to You
And our Father, above

Amen

Evening Prayer

As my day

Comes to an end
I pray for all
My family and friends

For health and joy

For love and peace
And for myself
A restful sleep

I thank You for

The day You made
And pray that tomorrow
Is as good as today

Amen